Changing from Boys to Men:

The Importance of Mentoring African American Boys

Eric T. Ferguson

Kingdom Builders Publications LLC

Eric T. Ferguson

Changing from Boys to Men:
Copyright © 2016 by Eric T. Ferguson
Kingdom Builders Publications

All rights reserved. No part of this book may be reproduced or transmitted in any form or by any means without written permission from the author.

ISBN:
Paperback: 978-0-692-72880-2
Library of Congress Control Number 2016943504
Photographer – Albert Lee
Cover Artist – Bernard Jackson
Cover Designer – LoMar Designs

Editors:
Kingdom Builders Publications Editorial Staff
Donald Lee

Printed in USA
Go to these websites:
www.kingdombuilderspublications.com

All Holy Scriptures are taken from the King James Version of the Bible unless otherwise stated.

CONTENTS

	Acknowledgments	iv
	Prologue	v
1	Mentor-the Acronym	8
2	Make Time to Make Mentoring…	13
3	Embrace the Responsibility…	23
4	Never Sugar-coat Perception…	26
5	Teach Respect for Women	30
6	Open and Honest Dialog…	34
7	React to Today's Social Climate…	39
8	When Times Get Tough…	43
9	Black Men Please Stand Up	46
	Epilogue	51
	References	54

ACKNOWLEDGMENTS

First and foremost, I give all praises to God for his grace and mercy upon my life. I thank God for what he has done, what he didn't do because it was for my good, and what he will do in my life as I continue this journey called life.

To my father and grandfather, the late Clarence Ferguson Sr., and the late Elder Isiah Ferguson Sr. for their love and direction. For working with their hands as a means of providing for their families and instilling in me the value of hard work, so that I could be afforded a life in which I can use my mind through education to achieve my goals in this life.

To my mother, my "Big" brother, and my aunts for guiding me in the best way they could during those years where I could have gone astray. I love you all more than words could ever express.

To my first mentee Jalan, who I have been matched with since 2005. We have gone through a lot, and I know that through it all we are both better for it. I am here for you forever, and look forward to seeing you pay it forward!

To all of my friends and family, mentees and mentors who have supported me in all I have done. I truly appreciate you all.

Last and certainly not least, to my family. Thanks you for all of your love and support, and for sharing me with others the way you have. I could not do what I do without that support. I love you.

PROLOGUE

The African-American community has long lived by the motto "*It takes a village to raise a child*," which is derived from an African proverb. The notions of being a *brother's keeper* and having each other's backs are perceived notions that symbolize commitment to ensuring that not even one person is left behind, regardless of his situation or circumstance. Sadly, African-American boys are being left behind, and in many ways cast aside. This is evident at the hand of other races, but more tragically this occurs within the Black race.

Mark 8:36 (NKJV) asks: "*For what would it profit a man if he gains the whole world, and loses his own soul?*" This is a question worth asking our Black men today. Is it okay if our biological children, (the only ones we are directly responsible for) are doing the right things? If they show respect and compassion for life, and others does it matter if their peers do not?

It is imperative that we make sure our homes are in order first. However, if we are doing nothing to reach those outside of our homes who are on the path toward crime, gangs, and other activities or those who have no male to view as a mentor, we are in essence sending our children into a society where values of obedience to the law, compassion for our fellow man, and respect for individuality and diversity are ignored. If we are going to eradicate crime and violence, particularly in the African-American community *(African Americans make up nearly 1 million of the 2.3 million incarcerated populations according to the NAACP Criminal Justice fact sheet)*, it is going to require getting involved in the mentoring of our African-American boys. If we do not, then the streets, television, and the Internet will. So many strong African- American women (who have taken on the roles of single handedly raising and developing these boys) are pleading for men of color to step up and provide the type of mentorship and guidance these boys need. Our women realize that they just do not have the capability or knowledge to give, as they have never been men. I lost my father at the age of fourteen and both of my grandfathers a few years later.

These men were strong figures in my life. I was blessed with a strong-willed mother and paternal aunts who did all they could to guide my development into manhood, but still neither of them had ever been a Black man. Thankfully I had mentors in my band directors who took extra time to provide me with the guidance I needed from a Black man's perspective at a time when I needed it most. Where would many other

Black men with similar or even varying stories such as mine be today without the influences of a strong mentor?

MENTOR – THE ACRONYN
Chapter One

Merriam Webster defines **mentoring** as giving advice and instruction to someone regarding the course or process to be followed. Therefore, a mentor is someone who facilitates this process in an effort to guide the course of the *mentee*, or someone who is mentored. This guide to mentoring boys in the African – American community is geared toward providing simple ways for African – American men to step up in their communities and take these boys under their wings, equipping them with the knowledge they will need to be positive contributors to society. The Bible teaches us in **Proverbs 4:7**(NKJV), *Wisdom is the principle thing; therefore get wisdom. And in all your getting, get understanding).* As one who has always desired wisdom, I have learned to ask God for knowledge in certain situations. Acquiring wisdom may mean that you have to go through some things that may be uncomfortable at times. There are times that the journey we are going on will be painful. Had the outcome been known, a different path would probably have been taken. African-American men can prevent the younger generation from making the same mistakes by sharing that wisdom.

It is essential that men of color are armed with tools and resources to help aide in the development of boys of color as they change from boys to men, both physically and mentally. I do not proclaim to be an *expert* regarding the phases of mentoring. However, I am a Black man, and the father of two boys and a daughter, whom I love and cherish dearly. So I asked myself the following questions while penning this work:

Would I allow my sons to bring home a friend he met at school to play video games, basketball, or watch television with and not worry about any negative practices being placed in his mind? Will this friend be the type of person who will help my son avoid the *appearance of evil* when I am not around?

If my daughter came home one day and said, "Dad, I'm in love with this guy and he wants to be your son-in-law," would I have full comfort and confidence in the available candidates from whom she has made her choice?

If you answer any of these questions with uncertainty or a resounding "No," then you can and should desire to make a difference. So many times when events occur in the African-American community, where Black males are treated unjustly, or have placed themselves in situations that cause the media to shine a negative light on them, the response is, "Oh my God… What a shame!" The situation that occurred is definitely a shame, but the greater shame in many of these cases is that no one intervened with enough consistency and passion in the young Black man's life at an early age to provide guidance from a Black man's point of view to deter the negative behaviors. Let's begin by discussing simple methods to aide in solving a major problem in our communities, while letting the world know that all lives matter.

Many of the lead stories in the media outlets highlight a crime or negative activity, where an African-American male has been involved in an incident either as the perpetrator or the victim. The overwhelming response much of the time is, "My, my, my…That's such a shame." But where was this concern when this person was a youth in your community, school, church or family? Better yet, where were you? The shame in many of these situations is the lack of intervention on the part of Black men who didn't take responsibility in some way for these young Black boys.

The first way to change our boys into men is to have a clear understanding of the role of a mentor. The approach must be, "Why not mentor?" as opposed to how, when, where, or who specifically to mentor. Many of our young Black males have no male influences in their families who are fit enough physically, mentally, or spiritually to give clear and consistent guidance. I remember the many times my mother tried her best to compensate for my father's absence with a stern, hard-hand approach, but she wasn't relating to me the way my father would have.

Over the next six chapters, I will break down each of the following principles of mentoring in acronym form, illustrating how such an important role can be done in simple, yet effective ways:

M – Make time to make mentoring meaningful

E – Embracing the responsibility of mentoring

N – Never sugar-coat society's perception of the Black male, while empowering our young Black males to change the narrative

T – Teach respect for women

O – Open and honest dialog with your mentee

R – React to today's social climate with hope for positive change

The reality is many Black men in our communities can make a difference by getting involved. It is my hope that this book will serve as a guide that will ignite those men to answer the charge, either as outlined or in their own ways.

The goal is to drive the desire and passion to mentor.

MAKE TIME TO MAKE MENTORING MEANINGFUL
Chapter Two

For mentoring to be meaningful, one key ingredient needed is time. Time, one of our most valuable but scarce resources, drives the entire mentoring process. It does no good to occasionally engage in mentoring, as the power and influence may be minimal. One who mentors must ensure that time is spent in order to cultivate and nurture relationships, trust, and respect. Each opportunity to reach our young Black males is valuable, as the presence of negativity is ever present around them. If we fail to take time to effectively mentor these boys, some other group will —particularly, the gangs in our communities.

Gangs are constantly recruiting members from all races, particularly young Black males who appear lost, unfocused, and unguided. Gang recruiters look for the signs: Disengaged students who are late to class and perform poorly, students who are constantly in detention or in-school suspension, and those who receive out-of-school suspension. Gangs do a good job of engaging these young black males by making them feel as if they are needed and valued. The mind is a seat of influence, and if one can gain control over another's thought process and deductive reasoning, then he can get that individual to do almost anything it desires. As we correlate this to mentoring and the importance of time, spending quality time with your mentee, thus sharing positivity and encouragement, can guide his thought process and reasoning skills, should he be faced with a situation that could result in a negative outcome.

There are numerous ways to spend time with your mentee that will have a meaningful result. Making the time spent meaningful requires "turning little moments, into big magic," as proclaimed by Big Brother Big Sisters of America. Committing time to mentor in your schedule is only a portion of the battle. Deciding how to best use this time is crucial. A few options to make mentoring time meaningful that I employ are discussed in the following sections.

Weekly Calls to Your Mentee

Life at times can be busy for everyone. Juggling work, family, and other responsibilities can result in time slipping away and a person merely just forgetting to handle tasks he sets out to complete or was required to do. Today's technology makes it easy to reach out and touch someone instantaneously regardless of distance or other prohibiting factors. I recommend setting up a reminder if needed via phone or e-mail each week that is designated for a fifteen-minute call with your mentee. Although sending an encouraging text message or e-mail is also a great way to stay in touch with your mentee, the effect of the verbal exchange will lead to a deeper, more effective relationship.

In these sessions, subscribe to the 80/20 rule, where you listen for 80 percent of the time so your mentee can express his thoughts, experiences, and feelings. You as the mentor should use the 20 percent of time providing feedback and positive direction on what was shared. This way, each party can leave the conversation with a clear understanding of what has been expressed and what actions to take going forward. With today's social media outlets, and text messaging, most of our youth rarely use the telephone to "speak" to someone on the other end. Although these fifteen-minute telephone sessions are in essence small fractions of time in a week, they can be used to detect issues, redirect behaviors and thoughts, and offer positive encouragement that will carry your mentee throughout the week. I have found this to be an effective tool when communicating with all of my mentees, but even more so with the ones without a male figure in their immediate family circle.

While this is set time for you and your mentee to touch bases, you want to always encourage open communication at all times with your mentee. Understand that their issues or concerns are not governed by your schedule. At times being mentor requires sacrifice, which means you may be needed, even when you are busy or didn't expect to be called upon to serve in your mentoring role. Be willing to attend to your mentee's needs with care and concern, as opposed to an attitude of being bothered or perceived as too busy. These actions will further build his bond with you, creating a trust in what is being shared. A mentor never wants to be viewed as someone who cannot be reached, or is too busy. Understand that if your mentee calls you, he feels a connection that he does not have with anyone else. Therefore, you should feel privileged to do all you can to address his concerns. Meeting him where his is, and making sure that he doesn't feel alone when faced with a circumstance that he doesn't feel totally comfortable addressing with only the knowledge he possesses is being a true mentor to the young Black male.

School Visits

Mentoring is a partnership. Again, "It takes a village to raise a child." At least once a quarter, a mentor should make the time to visit his mentee's school, to see his mentee interact in his learning environment. Take this time to see who he is associating with to determine the type of children with whom he interacts. Are these children paying attention in class or disruptive and talkative? Are these children peers who will help him stay on track or are they peers who will lead him to deviate from what he knows is right? These types of questions can be answered in these short, yet powerful visits by simply observing. Remember that as a mentor, you want your mentee to influence his peers in a positive manner so that they will behave positively. Never judge any of his peers in a negative way, as they may need mentoring, too.

School visits also mean partnering with your mentee's parents or guardians in order to be allowed to speak with teachers, coaches or guidance counselors to get their input on the progress being made and what actions, if any, need to be taken to correct behaviors. Gaining this type of access to the mentee's life shows a level of caring that will strengthen the bond you both share. This will eliminate the common question and answer segment of, "How are things in school going?" and your mentee responds with "Fine." The information gained from your school visits will lead to conversations that spark encouragement to continue on the current path or lead to redirecting poor behaviors that may be hindering his success.

This is merely a one-hour investment in time, at least once a quarter (more time or frequency may be required based on the mentee's progress), but the return on such a time investment in the life of the young man will pay great dividends. Your mentee will realize that you care about the steps he is taking to gain a quality education, something that no one can take from him. With the alarming statistics about young Black boys performing poorly in school (in comparison to their white counterparts), you as a mentor must make it your business to be involved and present in partnership with his parents or guardians so that his support system is strong, united, and always present. In Tavis Smiley's 2011 PBS piece _Too Important to Fail: Saving America's Boys_, it notes that 54 percent of African Americans graduate from high school, compared to more than three quarters of white and Asian students.

We cannot afford to have our young Black males

put into a box and limited as to what they can do with their skills and talents, just because they are Black. They must be encouraged to take full advantage of the educational opportunities as all others, and by being active in this aspect of their lives; you can help assure they are given the chances to attempt courses or programs that someone else may feel they're not suited for. Participating in the academic advisement of my own children, I found it disheartening to see many Black students go in for advisement alone and come out within ten minutes of entering the counselor's office. To me, it seems as if his destiny is being selected for him as opposed to him selecting his destiny. As a mentor, after your mentee's parents, grandparents, or guardians you should want to be a contact person on the school's calling list.

Spend time in faith settings/conversations with your mentee

I am one who firmly believes in the Word of God, and the purpose that God has for each of our lives. In mentoring young Black males, I think it is essential that time is spent focusing on this notion of God's purpose to prosper the lives of his children. Not prosperity in terms of riches and stature, but in terms of values, morals, and a desire to be of service to others. Spending time talking to your mentee about faith and his belief in God (or lack thereof) will help reinforce or even provide knowledge of God's word that he can tap into when decisions need to be made about whether to do what is morally right.

In spending time in faith with your mentee, you must be transparent with him so that your testimonies are *real*. Share with your mentee the fact that you have fallen short of the glory of God in some of your actions, but by His grace and mercy you were able to overcome mistakes and setbacks in your life. There will be times in your mentee's life where he will have to draw on his faith to see him through whatever valley in life he may face. Therefore, spending time discussing faith (including scriptures on comfort and strength) is a good way of spending time with your mentee. A few of my favorite scriptural references for encouragement are:

1. **Philippians 4:13** (NKJV) *I can do all things through Christ, who strengthens me.*

2. **Jeremiah 29:11** (NIV) *For I know the plans I have for you, declares the Lord. Plans to prosper you and not harm you. Plans to give you hope and a future.*

3. **Psalm 37:25** (AMP) *I have been young, and now I am old, yet I have not seen the righteous (those in right standing with God) abandoned or his descendants pleading for bread.*

4. **Proverbs 3:5-6** (NKJV) *Trust in the LORD with all your heart, and lean not on your own*

understanding; In all your ways acknowledge Him, And He shall direct your paths.

Of course, these are just a few of the numerous scriptures that can be referenced for encouraging, uplifting and reassuring our young Black males as they journey through life. The important thing is to know that the time you spend talking to your mentee on the power of faith will help him realize that no matter what may come his way, faith can sustain and elevate him in all situations, giving him a testimony to share with someone else for encouragement.

EMBRACE THE RESPONSIBILITY OF MENTORING
Chapter Three

Being a mentor is a key role to play in the development of our youth. That mentor is more than just an adult who comes around or who calls to "check in "once or twice a month. Mentors give a level of guidance and build trust that is very hard to breach. If the mentor, however, does not follow through with his commitment to the mentee in terms of support, time, encouragement and constructive feedback, the harm done to the youth can be life-altering in a negative way. For this reason, those who desire to mentor must embrace the full responsibility of molding this young person indefinitely.

Many of these boys have experienced the rejection of being left behind and forgotten by the men who were supposed to guide their paths and they need strong influences that will stay the course, even when the days are challenging. Embracing the role of a mentor and understanding its importance in the African-American community require a man who cares about something or someone else other than himself. A mentor must be someone who is selfless and understands that the race is not won by the swift, or the strong, but he who endures until the end, as the Word of God teaches us.

Understand, too, that there is no equation that will accurately allow you to predict the exact amount of time necessary to be an effective mentor. A huge aspect of embracing your role entails knowing that different situations require different measures. As the mentor, you have to obtain a level of knowledge and wisdom to be able to gauge how in depth you need to be on a matter so that your mentee gains the knowledge needed to successfully navigate his situation.

So why is mentoring a *Responsibility?* Well, mentoring allows you to directly affect the social deck in the favor of future generations contributing to our society as opposed to being irreversibly dependent upon it. One of my mentees is an intellectual genius who, despite all the support and opportunities he was given, would not apply his brilliance in the classroom. This young man's mother and guidance counselor just could not get him to realize the importance of completing assignments timely. The young man's mother called me one day to inform me that his lack of follow-through on school assignments had placed him in jeopardy of failing his grade. After getting that call, I immediately arranged to meet with my mentee later that day to further explain the severity of his situation and what consequences would result if his path did not change. This example illustrates the importance of the responsibility of mentoring.

A mentor must embrace the reality that what he says or does in mentoring has lasting effects on his mentee's decisions. This could be in many cases the difference between life and death, as many times our young Black males are faced with peer pressure and situations that lead to decisions that negatively impact their lives forever. Gangs and individuals who engage in illegal activities recruit those who don't have a visible support system. In embracing this responsibility, you will increase the probability of producing a Black man who will make positive contributions to our society. If you truly desire to be your brother's keeper, this concept is a no-brainer.

NEVER SUGAR-COAT PERCEPTION OF THE BLACK MALE
Chapter Four

As a mentor, you should never paint a picture or give the perception that in today's society young Black males are not viewed or portrayed as "*troubled*" or "*thugs*" or [arguably the most used adjective] "*at-risk youth*." All youth are at risk of something, if not properly nurtured, regardless of race or socio-economic status. Keeping it real, or *100*, on these perceptions will open up a dialogue with your mentee as to how you view Black males in society, and more importantly how your mentee can change any negative perception society may have by the actions he exhibits as a Black male.

Many of our misguided young Black males are driven by the actions that will give them what they deem as valuable *street credibility*. What is street credibility? It is gaining a reputation based on negative implications, which will not lead to anywhere positive! What type of backward thinking lunacy is that? It prevents one from being able to secure a decent job to provide for oneself because of a criminal record. It also may prevent one from being able to have a voice in democracy as a citizen, hinders him from being able to vote. That's keeping it 100 percent stupid! For this reason in itself, many of our young Black males in our communities have not only failed themselves, but all those who have prayed for them and the others who will never benefit from the true skills and talents these young Black males possess. These are the truths that must be expressed to your mentee directly, with no filters. Our young Black males need to understand that the reality is many in our society have *awarded* them the superlative l*east likely to succeed.*

As you empower your mentee to change society's perception of the Black male, encourage him to focus on the following two points:

Be what you want to be viewed as a Black male.

As a young Black male, you do not want to be viewed as having no purpose or direction, or being *at risk*. Therefore, in your thoughts and actions, make sure you conduct yourself in a manner that promotes your self-worth, portrays a vision to strive to succeed, and shows respect for life and others in society despite our various differences. Encourage your mentee to surround himself with peers who desire to be successful in life, through work and preparations knowing that nothing will be given, and that the harvest to be reaped from this will last longer than those things that are just handed to him. Our young Black males must understand that no one owes them anything.

Young Black males, understand that the actions you take, whether positive or negative, are owned solely by you. There are factors that may put you at a disadvantage such as physical surroundings, lack of means, and lack of guidance from individuals charged with your rearing. However, ultimately rising above and beyond any impediments lies within you. The one "Man" holding you back is the one you see in the mirror. Make him great through your works!

Understand that if it's not right, it's wrong, regardless of how popular it may be.

Human nature draws one to the crowd of acceptance, where it appears people are having more fun and joy. As a mentor, never lose focus on stressing to your mentee that being a part of the in-crowd is not always a good thing. The *in-crowd or cliques* are comprised of various opinions, views, ideologies, and reasoning processes that can lead to making decisions that under normal circumstances, one would respond to differently. Based on the company your mentee keeps, he can be encouraged to make positive choices that will propel him to greater levels in life, or he can succumb to poor decisions that can derail his path. Your job as a mentor is to help him understand the difference.

Positive peer engagement leads to conversations about goals and aspirations to provide for one's self and the community. Negative peer engagement, however, leads to those conversations and actions that yield hurt and harm to those communities we live in and inhibit prosperity. Your actions are not society's perceptions of you; these actions reflect you defining for everyone to see who you have chosen to be. **1 Corinthians 15:33** NIV *"Do not be misled: Bad company corrupts good character."*

TEACH RESPECT FOR WOMEN
Chapter Five

One of the most important concepts you must convey to your mentee is the importance and necessity of respecting women. The ways we teach our Black boys to speak to females from a young age is crucial to the ways in which they will communicate with them as they grow into maturity.

One way to achieve this is to encourage our boys to view females as partners, not as subordinates. It is important that young Black males are taught that they are by nature, charged with leading, serving, nurturing, and protecting our women in a loving way. However, we must not encourage a sexist attitude in which women are viewed as beneath men. Those types of views will yield interactions that project those views. Such interactions can lead to other ways in which women are not respected, including men committing acts of domestic violence against women.

According to the article *<u>30 Shocking Domestic Violence Statistics That Remind Us It's An Epidemic,</u>*

(2014 The Huffington Post), 4,774,000 women in the United States experience physical violence from intimate partners every year. In the African-American community, it is reported that Black females in 2011 were murdered by Black male intimate partners at a rate of 2.61 per 100,000 females, while white women were murdered at a rate of 0.99 per 100,000 white females. What if some man put his hands on your mother, daughter, sister, niece, etc.? What would your reaction be? You must convey the passion of these questions to your mentee in a way that the mere thought of committing such an act would be felt as inhumane, because it is.

Multiple studies conducted by The Violence Policy Center in 2013, the vast majority of homicides of Black females happened in the course of an argument with a Black male partner. Our Black boys must be taught from an early age the importance of respect for females' in relation to conflicts, and the need for a resolution that is respectable. Mentors, help your mentees understand that committing violence against girls or women has no positive gains nor does it prove any point of masculinity. At a time in our society where domestic violence is increasing year by year, mentors must encourage and talk to the mentees about the importance of avoiding situations where this can occur. Love is respect and doesn't cause physical hurt. Anyone who has been in a relationship understands that emotions are deeply involved that can cause joy and pain mentally. The value of one's dignity and life must mean more to a person than physically hurting a woman because of such emotions.

Our young Black males must be shown the value in respecting women, especially if they have no model to follow due to absence in the home or family circle. Being a mentor will require leading by example. In interacting with your mentee, explain and exhibit the behaviors of respect. Simple steps such as opening and holding doors, allowing females to sit first, standing up to pull out the chair as a female approaches the table, are all examples of action that convey respect for women. By exposing our Black boys to such behaviors, you are arming them with valuable traits that can lead to more actions of compassion and care that can translate to other situations in their lives.

Developing in our young Black males the mentality of respect for women can sometimes be challenged, due to factors such a television, Internet and music. As with many of our daily avenues of entertainment or enjoyment, these entities have tremendous value. However, when the concepts that promote a lack of respect for women are conveyed via these mediums, the challenge grows. Our women should not be portrayed or referred to in derogatory forms. It is imperative that our young Black males understand the difference between artistic creativity and freedom, as my point is not to pass any judgment on that. However, when art is absorbed as life, it can form dangerous views and ideologies that in ways promote devaluing women based on such expressions. In other words, with great freedom comes great responsibility.

For me personally, there is no one, nor will there ever be anyone like my "Momma," who sacrificed so much for me. To add to that, my paternal aunts who stood in the gap to ensure I had all the support needed to grow into maturity mean everything to me. The question must be posed: Mentees, would you want someone to refer to the most important women in your life in disrespectful ways? I want our young Black males to embrace this sentiment of respect. Instead of degrading overtures, our young Black males must be taught to realize that if they in any way threaten or actually put their hands on a female violently, they are in no way a man.

OPEN AND HONEST DIALOGUE WITH YOUR MENTEE
Chapter Six

Our young Black males can see through any fake images anyone may try to put on to impress, or use to engage them. Therefore, from the onset, a good mentor should always be open and honest. The focus of a mentor should be to positively influence the life of the mentee so that he is able to achieve his purpose in life. As I stated earlier, wisdom and knowledge are both essential to the development of our young Black males (wisdom comes by experiences, while knowledge is gained from heeding to and applying the advice given to one's situation). By being open and honest with your mentee, you can decrease the undue pains he can experience later in his life.

The open and honest dialogue shows a level of transparency in terms of your feelings, fears, and faults. By acknowledging your shortcomings and, more importantly, applying the steps you are taking to overcome them, you will build a strong bond with your mentee. The reality is that no one is a finished product. We are growing each day to become better human beings. This should be the goal of everyone. Young Black males need to see someone who looks like them with similar life stories as theirs that can share the testimony that a Black man can be a success, despite any obstacle that arises.

Again, success should not to be only gauged by worldly standards such as material wealth or accumulation of possessions, for there are many individuals with wealth that they will never be able to spend or whose moral compass is not visible. On the other hand, there are many others of meager means economically whose lives' are governed by solid values, morals, and compassion.

Young Black males need to see that making mistakes or facing challenging circumstances does not have to mean they are destined for failure in life. Being an open book with your mentee will allow him to see that mistakes do not have to define you. Many Black men have overcome poor decisions they have made, growing up in environments of poverty and crime, inadequately funded educational systems, and diminished economic opportunities. But through their perseverance and dedication to hard work, they were able to evaluate themselves despite these obstacles. As a youth, my mother advised me all the time about being in the company of the wrong people. She would term it "guilt by association."

One afternoon my junior year of high school, I took my mother's car without permission to give a family member a ride to a neighboring town because he needed to "get something." This family member asked me to turn down a side road, and then he got out and walked to the front door of a house. Within 2 minutes, he exited the home and returned to the car. As we turned onto the main highway to return home, two police cars pulled up behind us. So I pulled over, not thinking anything was wrong. I wasn't speeding and I used the proper turn signal.

The reason for the stop, however, was because the house my family member entered and exited quickly had been under surveillance for drug activity.
Immediately the officers had both of us to get out of the car and they began to pat us down and search my mother's car. As the situation unfolded and after an hour of being held in the police car, the officers allowed me to call my mother, who sent a family friend to go and get me and take me home. The police let me go because they believed that I was just in the wrong place at the wrong time, i.e., naïve to what had transpired. It was discovered that my family member did have a small amount of Crack in a match box and was detained. All I saw as I sat in

the back seat of that patrol car was my dreams of college and a future gone. Not to mention the shame and disappointment that would be placed on my mother and family. But because of God's grace and mercy, I avoided the life derailment, but definitely not the wrath of a mother who I disobeyed!

One final point regarding open and honest communication: Never assume your mentee "knows certain things" just because you perceive it to be common knowledge. Assume that he does not know, unless you have armed him with the knowledge. At times, this will require you to re-emphasize information, even if the concept or topic you are discussing seems to be one that any reasonable person would comprehend.

With the race disparity amongst the number of young Black boys not finishing high school (various studies range between as much as 20 – 30 percent behind their White counterparts), committing crimes and joining gangs and being raised by single mothers, the knowledge-sharing portion of mentoring must be done with a no-holds-barred mentality because we are losing too many of our young Black males senselessly. As it is says in **Hosea 4:6**, "*My people perish for lack of knowledge.*"(KJV) We must arm our young Black males with real-world, life-sustaining knowledge that can be applied to their everyday lives.

Eric T. Ferguson

REACT TO TOADY'S SOCIAL CLIMATE WITH HOPE AND PRAYER TO POSITIVE CHANGE
Chapter Seven

As a mentor, at times it may be emotionally challenging and even seem idiotic or utopic to believe that society will change, and that a Black man can be treated equally in comparison to his white counterpart in today's world. Trayvon Martin, Michael Brown, Eric Garner, Walter Scott, Freddie Gray, Jonathan Ferrell — all Black males, among the countless others killed by the hands of others when their lives did not have to end.

Although each of these cases had a differing variable, and escalated for different reasons, the fact remains that the end result could have been avoided. So, how do we tell our young Black males with conviction that all lives matter while personally having doubts as these atrocities continue to occur in our society to those who look like them in the second decade of the 21stcentury?

These tragic occurrences in many ways have polarized America, as strong opposing views and opinions have been expressed. Many have doubts that jurisprudence still has its place in our society, especially when those who are behind the shield of the law are seen as getting away with the murdering of Black males. I personally believe this is where one's faith must come into play to evoke the sentiment of hope for our future, even in troubled times such as these.

Based on past and present patterns and practices that occur every day, as a disproportionate number of young Black males are involved in profiling situations of traffic stops, searches, and use of excessive force by law enforcement, young Black males feel a target has been placed on them, and every move they make is being magnified to "catch" them doing something wrong. A 2014 article in the Washington Post highlighted the following statistics gathered from federal statistics:

"Black drivers are 31 percent more likely to be pulled over than whites; they are more than twice as likely to be subject to police searches as white drivers; and they are nearly twice as likely to not be given any reason for the traffic stop."

A 2015 study in The Guardian highlighted the following statistics in regards to Black males versus White males when it comes to excessive force used:

"Despite making up only 2 percent of the total US population, African American males between the ages of 15 and 34 comprised more than 15 percent of all deaths logged this year by an ongoing investigation into the use of deadly force by police. Their rate of police-involved deaths was five times higher than for white men of the same age."

As a mentor, you have the power to react to these actions by encouraging your mentee to make wise decisions. Although there is no guarantee that profiling will not occur, avoiding those places or situations where bad things tend to happen is one way to improve the chances of not being accosted. Explain to your mentee that his actions and reactions in such situations can instigate some of the negative reactions he may receive. Our young Black males must understand that being in places that they do not belong will create situations where the light will shine brighter in their direction, and make it easier to be profiled.

You can ask, "What do you do when you are not in places that will attract trouble, and because of the color of your skin you are subjected to those situations where someone else's ignorance can affect your life? "Our young Black males must be taught the importance of making it home safely. It is sad that we have to suggest to a mentee, in this day and age where everyone is supposed to be free, that he may have to compromise those freedoms just to see another day. The only way a change will come is if we are alive to make that change.

Therefore, mentees conform to what law enforcement is requesting of you without confrontation so that you are able to return to your home safely. This is the only way you can help make the changes needed in the future.
It is no secret that young Black males have been one of,

if not the most negatively scrutinized and stereotyped group in America. I believe many of these stereotypes have been over-perpetuated by the media based on the music they listen to, their clothing styles and hairstyles, etc. Our boys are so much more than these perceptions. Sadly, instead of probabilities of the number of young Black males who will graduate high school by eighteen years old, we are able to readily find more studies or reports that outline the probabilities of this demographic being incarcerated, and for various levels of different crimes. As a mentor, you must react to such perceptions of our society by empowering your mentee to write the story he wants to be told through his integrity, character, personal, and public conduct.

The key is to promote behaviors in your mentee that will facilitate his achievement of the goals he sets for himself. Although the hopes and prayers of mentees' families for their lives are not to be devalued, the vision being pursued must satisfy your mentee first and foremost. Always ask your mentee "What do you want your life to look like?" and make sure you empower him to take the necessary steps to achieve this.

WHEN TIMES GET TOUGH DON'T GIVE UP
Chapter Eight

I have laid out some steps to mentoring that will make the process effective. But what do you do when the efforts you make do not produce the results you believe in your heart they should? What about when you know that you have given the needed effort, time, and guidance to help develop your mentee, but his actions are not in line with the wisdom you have imparted? Please, do not give up. In mentoring, just as in raising my own children, I have come to realize that one approach will not work with each individual. Therefore, mentors must adapt their styles and methods of reaching our young Black males based on where they are as individuals. In mentoring, I have seen my mentees grow from young boys to adolescents and then teenagers, where their focus in school, behaviors at home, and overall demeanor had changed in a way that I never thought would be imaginable at times. I thought this would never happen with any of my mentees because I felt that I did everything right in my mentorship.

Getting that call from a mentee's parent stating that your mentee has been disrespectful at home, or is doing poorly academically, or is displaying poor conduct in school will make you evaluate everything you have said to your mentee, especially when you are able to see him after getting in trouble, and the response you get is one of lack of concern or even nonchalance. At these points, a mentor has to humble himself, and realize that the focus must be solely on the young man, because he needs that mentor's support more than ever. And there are times when a mentor's tone of disappointment or even his act of chastisement should be minimal. Mentors must be there for the days their mentees receive awards, as well as the days they receive reprimands. Consistency is the key, and in time it will pay off. The goal is for the mentor's mentee to be a positive contributor in society. Again, success is measured in various ways, not just in the amount of degrees or titles one accumulates.

Giving up when issues arise does not represent mentors' charge of helping our young Black boys' transition into manhood. This would be quitting, which cannot be an option. Our young Black boys must be allowed to fall at times, and be assured that the helping hands of Black men will be there to pick them up, and help them get back on track. This is where both sides must refocus and reconnect on what the mentee sees as his future, and how he plans to achieve this. The aspirations in life may change over time. In the earlier years, college, for example, may have been the path. However, as time has passed, one's mentee may come to realize that traditional school is not for him, and that getting a vocation or trade would be in his best interest in order to be a productive citizen. Celebrate his choice and try your best to assist him in all ways possible. As long as your mentee desires to secure a job or career that is honest, offer your support.

Also, the mentee must be taught how to handle failure. It's important for him to know that we all fall short of the mark at some point. This is crucial to the development of the mentee. When failure occurs, one's mentee must be encouraged to learn from what occurred and take the steps necessary not to make the same mistakes again. Mentors, teach your mentees to understand that failure is not the end, but that failure builds understanding when the lessons learned are applied to his actions going forward.

Mentoring is not easy by any means, and you will have to adapt and adjust as time passes, but the lasting effects of a mentor's effort can do so much for our communities as a whole.

BLACK MEN PLEASE STAND UP
Chapter Nine

The need for men of color to be active mentors to our young is ever apparent. Many have suggested that the young Black male be listed as an endangered species, categorized as *at risk* of dropping out of school, committing crimes, joining gangs, going to jail, or fathering and then bastardizing children because this is what they have been exposed to. Our young Black males have been viewed as *endangered species*, because of the disproportionate use of excessive force on young Black males by law enforcement in our society that has been allowed to continue killing young Black males far too often. As referenced previously in this guide, young Black males are 31 percent more likely to be pulled over by the police, and five times more likely to be involved in police involved deaths than young White males.

In education, which serves as a gateway to opportunity in life, our Black boys are at risk of being endangered in many ways due to the lack of funding for education in many communities of color, where high poverty and unemployment exist. In a 2008-2009 analysis conducted by the

Department of Education, findings revealed that *"High poverty schools received less than their fair share of state and local funding, leaving students in high poverty schools with fewer resources than schools attended by wealthier peers."* The findings from the Department of Education went on to say *"The data reveal that more than 40 percent of schools that receive federal Title I money to serve disadvantaged students spent less state and local money on teachers and other personnel than schools that don't receive Title I money at the same grade level in the same district."* This lack of spending on those who are charge in developing our boys may affect the quality of the teachers and personnel, and efforts they put forth due to the compensation and support received. In a report done in 2011 from NEA Today with analysis from the National Education Association (NEA), the following telling points were made:

• Poor teacher salaries combined with low overall funding leads to difficulty recruiting and retaining educators other than those who are new to the profession, or those who couldn't find jobs anywhere else
• On average, schools with low-income students have fewer veteran teachers who are at the top of the salary scale. Some stay, but others burn out in the high-stress environment and transfer to more affluent schools with better resources.
• As a result, higher paid, more experienced

teachers wind up in more affluent schools, and lower-paid, less qualified teachers wind up at low income schools, triggering a cycle of inequity.

Although these are sad realities in our society, this mindset of being endangered gives the perceptions that there is limited hope for young Black males, and with this categorization, I firmly disagree, as we have the power to change these circumstances by being actively involved in our communities. I disagree because my personal story, like many others, is different because of mentors — strong Black men in my life and community — that realized their charge to be the *village* I needed. I was shown through my mentors that there was a whole world of opportunity for me away from my small-town surroundings. These same views can be shared with young Black males in any community in the inner city, suburbs, or country roads. My village showed me that if I was willing to work hard, put in the time to gain knowledge, that I could achieve whatever I desired in life. That is the power of mentorship — the power to encourage someone along his journey toward his goals and desired plan for success.

I was taught that crime and dishonesty would never prevail and that if I ever wanted anything sustainable, that it was not going to appear overnight. My grandfather, a Southern preacher who also had land on which he farmed, always talked to me about working hard and smart, and that in due season, we would reap the harvest. I asked him as a young boy what that meant. He replied, **Galatians 6:9** - *"So let's not get tired of doing what is good. At just the right time we will reap a harvest of blessings if we don't give up."* (NLT)

So why aren't more men of color stepping up to mentor our young Black boys? Is it the perception that those of a certain socioeconomic class are not wanted as mentors, hindering good Black men from stepping up to this charge of responsibility? What does that matter? As I have stated previously, I personally have been blessed to have my father and grandfathers active in my life during those formative years until their passing. The values of faith, family, respect for honest work, and the need to obtain a quality education were embodied in me by these men of minimal worldly treasures. But not everyone has this type of support system.

The reality is that there are *too many dead fathers, and not enough living relative*s in our communities. *Dead* in terms of the inactivity regarding taking on their responsibilities of being fathers to their sons. Some Black men have allowed situations and conflict with their children's mothers over custody and financial support and feelings of inadequacy to prevent them from participating in the *training-up* process of their children. They're *dead* in terms of not providing a loving, nurturing environment for their sons by spending time, sharing wisdom and experiences, providing guidance and direction in their lives. They're *dead* because all they do is work to ensure they provide the financial security needed to sustain a household. I was able to share some experiences with my father in our fourteen years together. *Hard worker and provider* are words that best describe the type of man my father was. These are great qualities. However, in rearing my own children, I want my descriptive terms to be *present, active in our li*ves, and *counselor.*

Not enough living relatives references the many able-bodied men who can fill the void in young Black boys' lives because of the inactivity of their fathers, but choose not to do so. Hopefully no one intentionally signs a lease, acquires a mortgage, or enrolls his children in a school where a community has no desire to prosper. Although all communities are not in affluent parts of town, all communities do have hard-working residents with values and morals who can offer their time and talents to aid in the development of these young Black boys. There is no true cost except time. This investment of time in the lives of these young Black boys has the potential for such an infinite return on one's investment.

EPILOGUE

I firmly feel that our communities have far too many capable villagers to pass these mentor-less Black boys by. Again I pose the question to all Black men asked in **Mark 8:36;** *For what will it profit a man, if he gains the whole world, and loses his own soul?"(NKJV)* Is it okay if only those we are directly responsible for are doing the right things and making sound choices that will impact their futures, even if their peers are not?

Black men, this a true call to action that we can no longer allow to go unanswered. This "Call to Action" catch phrase has been screamed so many times for so long. But what will it take for our society to truly act and get involved in the mentoring of African-American boys? The young African-American male is the target of such negative stereotyping and prejudgment that he needs a strong Black man who has in many ways overcome, despite these negativities. The power of mentoring can truly change these boys into men — men who will add substantive value to our society through their efforts, perspectives, visions, and most importantly their willingness to pay forward to the next generation the wisdom and knowledge they have obtained through having been mentored themselves. As Fredrick Douglas once said, "It is easier to build strong children than to repair broken men". Black men must stand up now!

Although this guide is geared toward encouraging and promoting Black men as mentors, I do want to acknowledge the efforts of those who are not Black men who take time out to mentor Black boys, as cultural competency is very important in our society. Cultural competency serves as a great benefit in improving cross-cultural effectiveness. It helps people from other races and backgrounds to able to understand the views, patterns, and ideologies of those different from themselves. Black men cannot get upset or harbor negative feelings when they see non-Black male figures mentoring Black boys, if they are unwilling to make the effort, themselves.

Mentorship of African-American boys should be viewed as a ministry. It should be seen as a means to reach those who are lost, those who need direction and motivation to stay on the right path. So if it is to be a ministry, I pose a very pointed question: Are we the keepers of the *village*, the capable Black men who live and work in communities, going to be "church folks?" Or are we going to be *Christians*? Church folks, in this sense, talk about the importance of mentoring when the bright lights and cameras are on, but when the lights are turned off and the fanfare diminishes, they disappear. When I say *Christians*, I am speaking in the sense that when the job needs to be done, and the need for mentoring is evident, there is more than talking about the need and value, but they are going to put in the work to make it a vital part of their lives. They make the necessary sacrifices when only they, the youth they mentor, and their God know what has been said or done.

A mentor understands the importance of

establishing a valuable connection with the mentee, not one who gets caught up in the pomp and circumstance of photo ops. As it has often been said, the true character of a person is revealed through his actions when no one is watching.

The concept of *each one, teach one* must be employed by African-American men toward our boys. These boys are needed to become men who will lead families, support our women in their efforts and visions, raise and mentor children who others will gravitate to in a positive way, and contribute productively to our society with their given talents. This is how we build up, maintain, and elevate the Black community. **Proverbs 22:6** says to *Train up a child in the way he should go: and when he is old, he will not depart from it. (KJV)* That, my brothers and sisters, is truly the meaning of being *My brother's keeper!*

Works Cited

- Sugarmann, Josh. "Black Women Face a Greater Risk of Domestic Violence." Huffington Post. Huffpost, 24 Oct. 13. Web. 25 Feb. 2015.
<http://www.huffinigtonpost.com/Black-women-face>.

- Vagianos, Alanna. "30 Shocking Domestic Violence Statistics That Remind Us It's an Epidemic." Huffington Post. Huffpost Women, 23 Oct. 2014. Web. 25 Feb. 2015.
<www.huffingtonpost.com%2F%2F2014%2F10%2F23%2Fdomestic.violence.statistics>.

- "The Violence Policy Card- When Men Murder Women." VCP Resources and Information. Violence Policy Center, Sept. 2013. Web. 25 Feb. 2015.
<http://www.vcp.org/>.

- Thompson, Tamika. "Fact Sheet: Outcomes for Young, Black Men." PBS. The Smiley Group, Inc., 2013. Web. 24 Feb. 2016.
<http://www.pbs.org/wnet/tavissmiley/tsr/too-important-to-fail/fact-sheet-outcomes-for-young-black-men/>.

- Ingraham, Chistopher. "You Really Can Get Pulled over for Driving While Black, Federal Statistics Show." The Washington Post. Wonkblog, 9 Sept. 2014. Web. 24 Feb. 2016.
<https://www.washingtonpost.com/news/wonk/wp/2014/09/09/you-really-can-get-pulled-over-for-driving-

while-black-federal-statistics-show/>.

- *Swaine, Jon, Oliver Laughland, Jamiles Larty, and Ciara McCarthy. "Young Black Men Killed by US Police at Highest Rate in Year of 1,134 Deaths." The Guardian. Guardian News and Media, 31 Dec. 2015. Web. 24 Feb. 2016.* *<http://www.theguardian.com/us-news/2015/dec/31/the-counted-police-killings-2015-young-black-men>.*

- *Long, Cindy. "How Do We Increase Teacher Quality in Low-Income Schools?" Nea Today. National Education Association, 24 May 2011. Web. 24 Feb. 2016.* *<http://neatoday.org/2011/05/24/how-do-we-increase-teacher-quality-at-low-income-schools/>.*

- *Criminal Justice Face Sheet | NAACP. Web. 28 Mar. 2016.* *www.naacp.org* *–pages-criminal-justice*

www.ingramcontent.com/pod-product-compliance
Lightning Source LLC
Chambersburg PA
CBHW062105290426
44110CB00022B/2719